Native American Horses

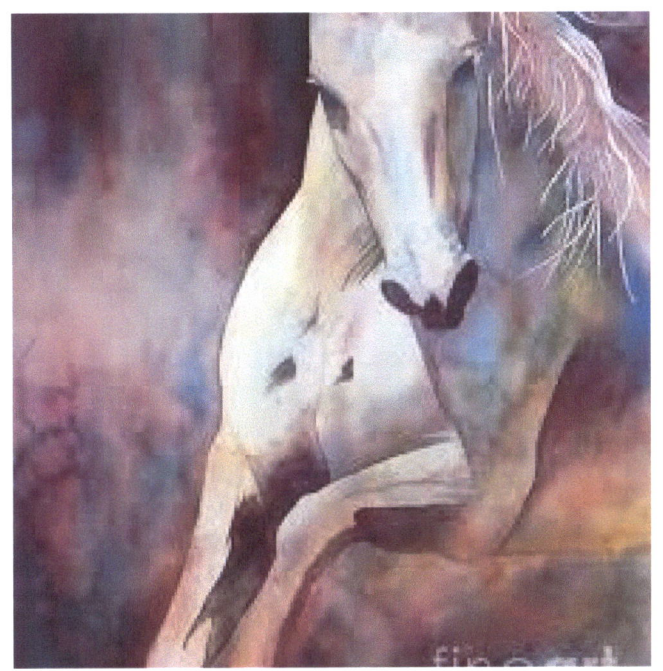

By Gene Allen Groner

Acknowledgements

The beautiful white horse on the title page is by Robert Hooper, word-renowned and award-winning artist.

Robert Hooper is an American watercolorist born in Yokosuka, Japan. He is pursuing his career in Fine Arts here in the United States. His award winning watercolors are exhibited in select Fine Art Shows and Gallerie s in the state of Arizona, where he currently resides with his family. As a young child growing up in Japan, Robert lived near Sankeien Gardens in Okohama, where he spent many of his days, feeding koi and looking for tadpoles in the lotus pond. Much of his inspiration today comes from recollecting images and experiences from this garden. During his school years, he was always fascinated with drawing and pencil sketching and became inspired by the paintings at his school art shows. Working with pencil and colored pencils, he learned the fundamentals which prepared him to discover the magic of watercolors! It is the only medium that 'moves'and inspires him today. 'There's nothing like painting withwatercolors because the light source is already there, and it shines through the paint from underneath! The luminosity and the transparency is uniquely watercolor' Robert is a self-taught artist, and feels the purest understanding of his own style must come through his own experimentation. His distinctive style of watercolor painting, using an intense and fluid palette, both on paper and canvas blends realism and abstract with spirit, energy, and serenity. His recent watercolor paintings on Arches paper is a layer on layer color application of the primaries with a brush and usually with no mix of colors. The paintings are framed and displayed behind glass. His watercolors on canvas are more abstract with a spontaneous and loose application of color. The watercolor paint is applied not with the brush contacting the surface, but with splatter, pouring and spraying using a hard bristle brush. This technique allows layering without the rush 'lifting' the layer below and also the use of more different and opaque colors. The canvas paintings are displayed in a gallery wrap presentation and the surface is sealed with a UV and moisture protection fixative.

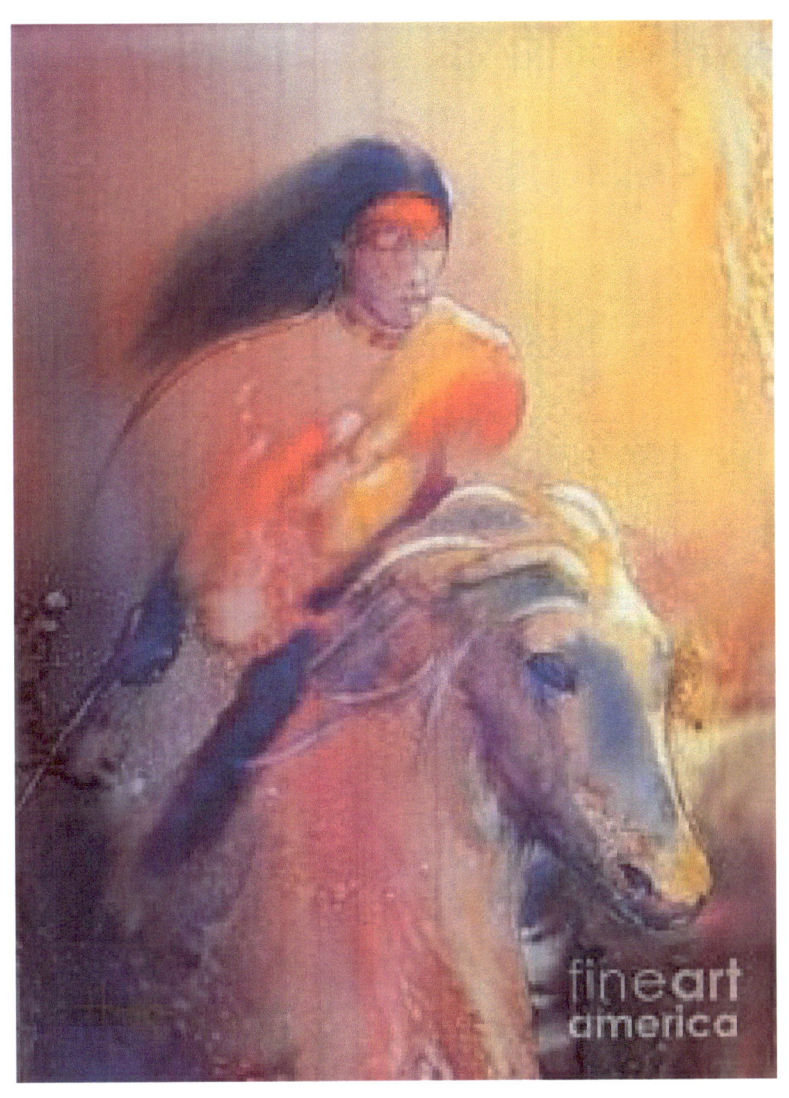

Fire Horse

Robert Hooper

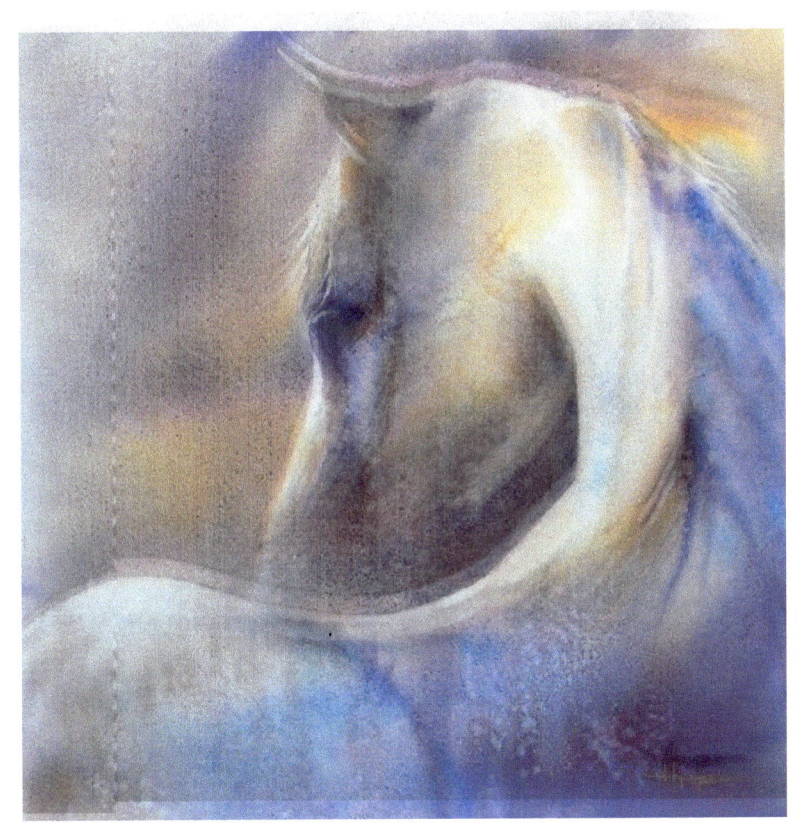

All My Relations

Robert Hooper

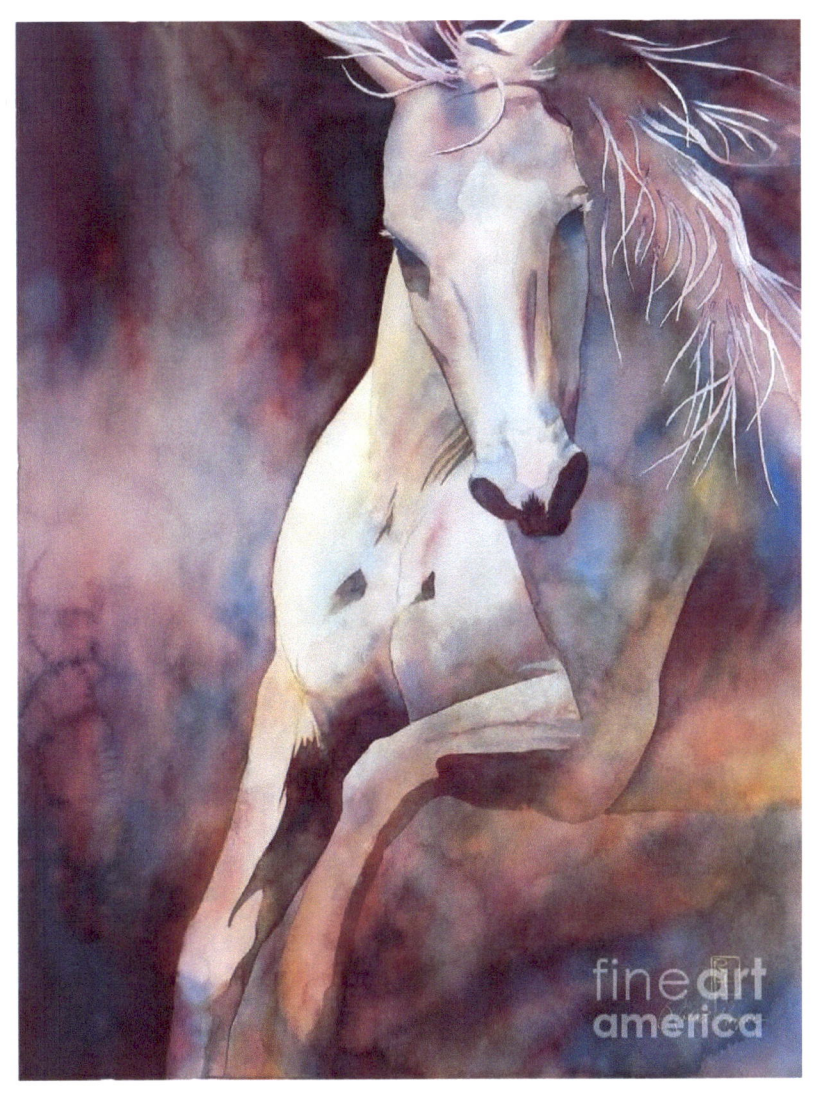

Spirit

Robert Hooper

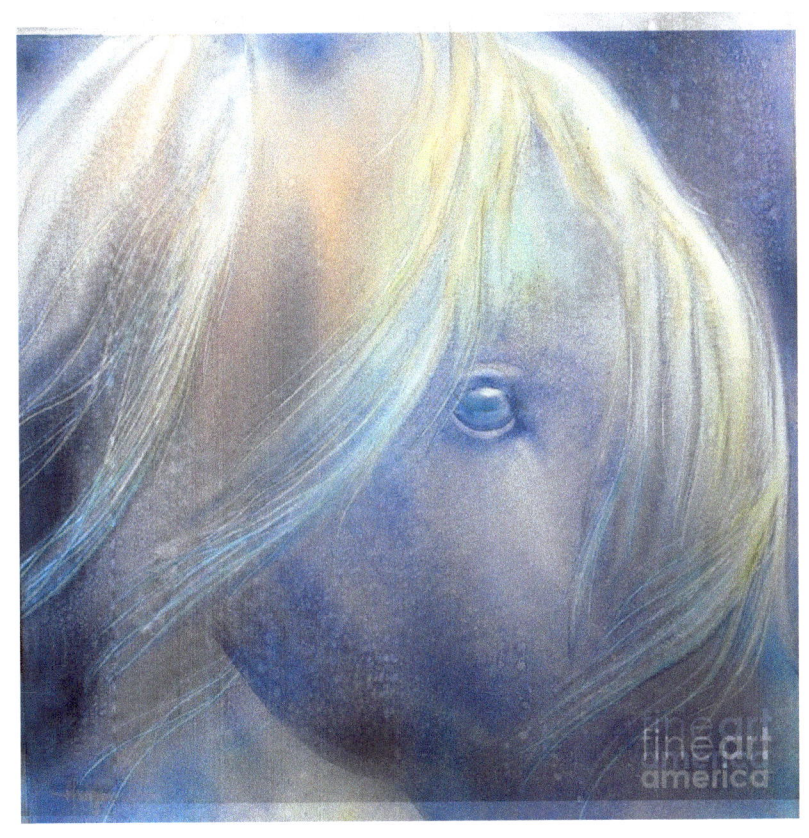

Spirit Horse

Robert Hooper

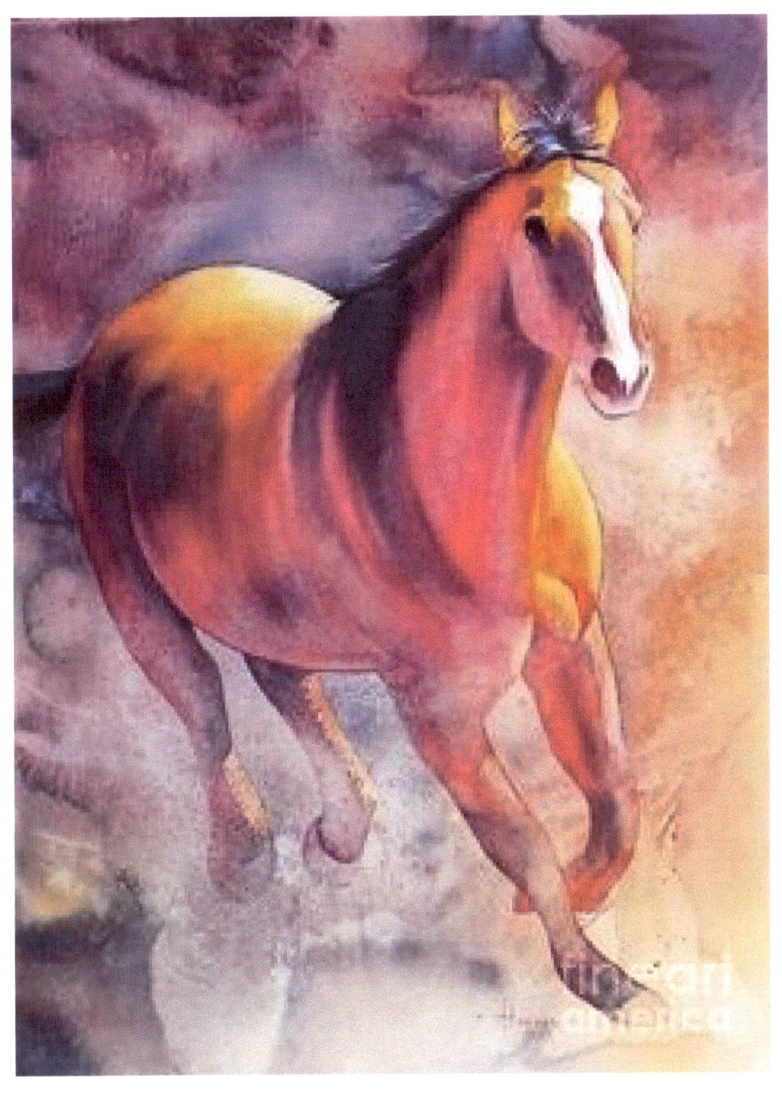

Running from the Storm

Robert Hooper

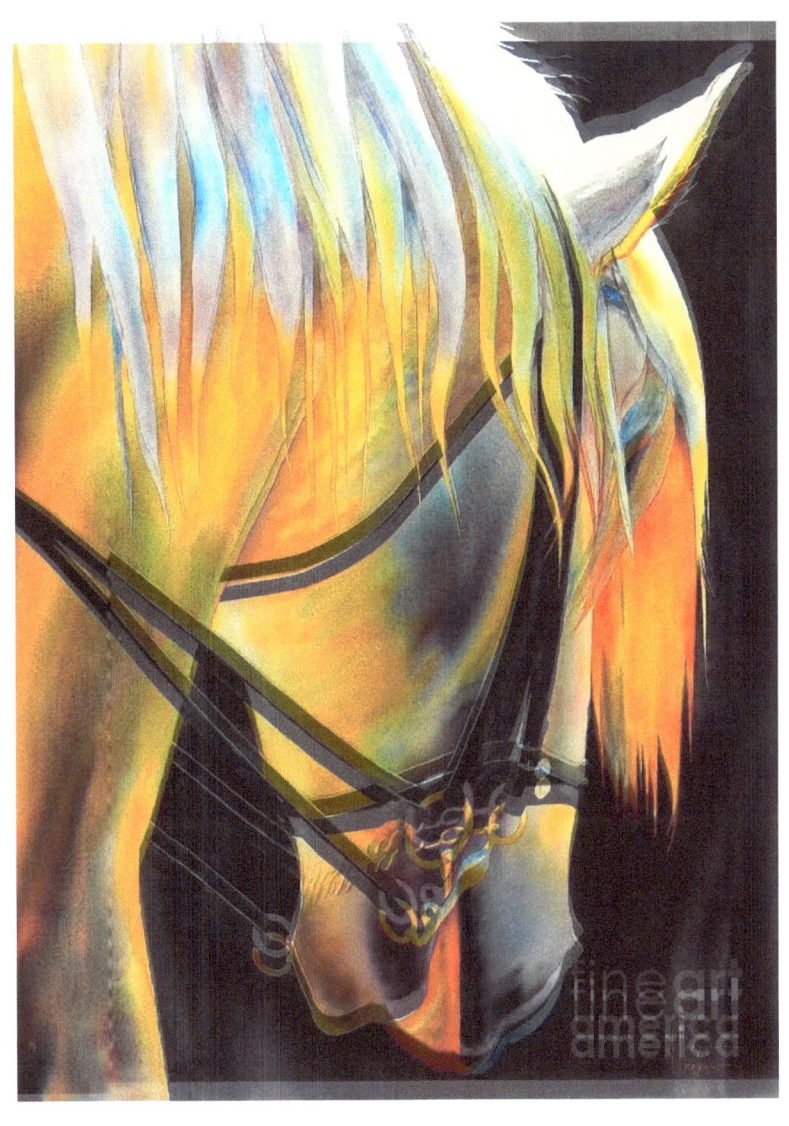

White Horse

Robert Hooper

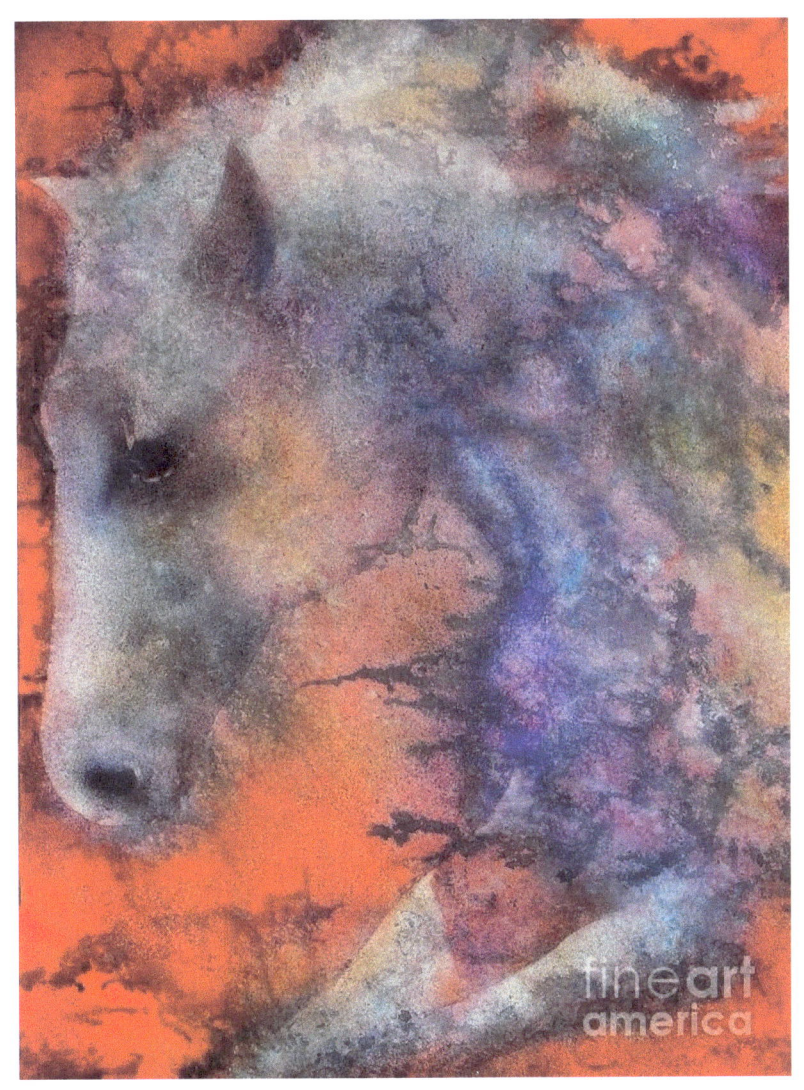

Wind Horse

Robert Hooper

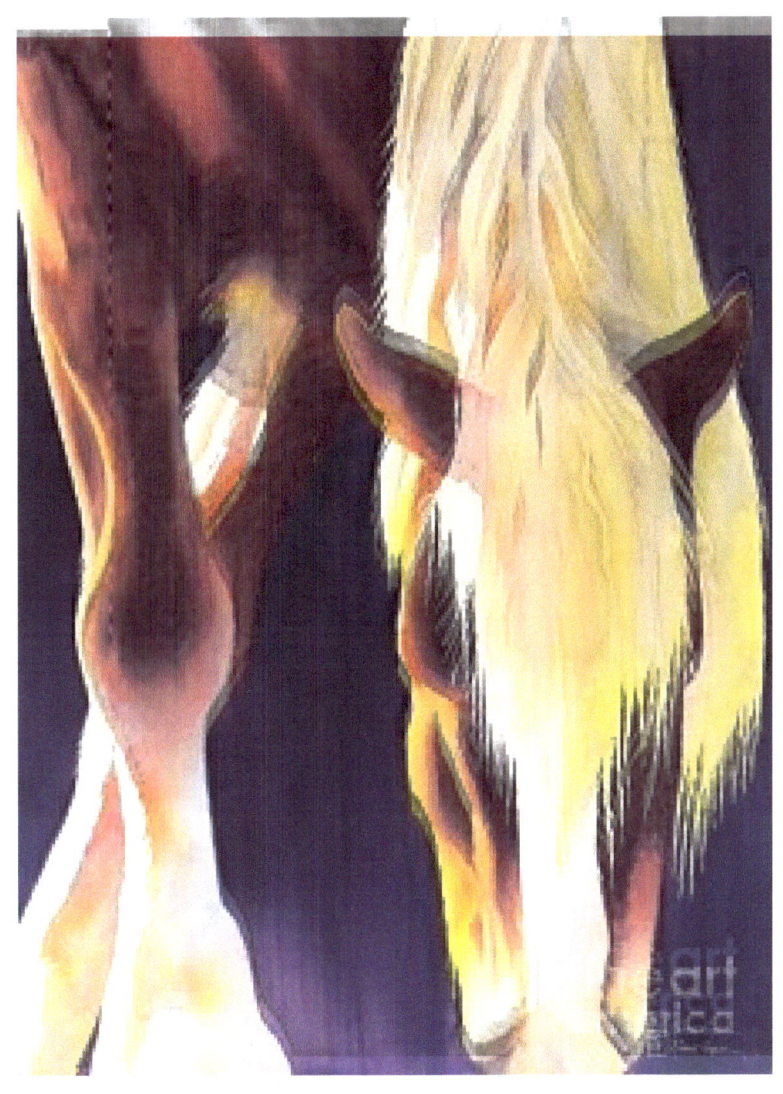

Eat Like a Horse

Robert Hooper

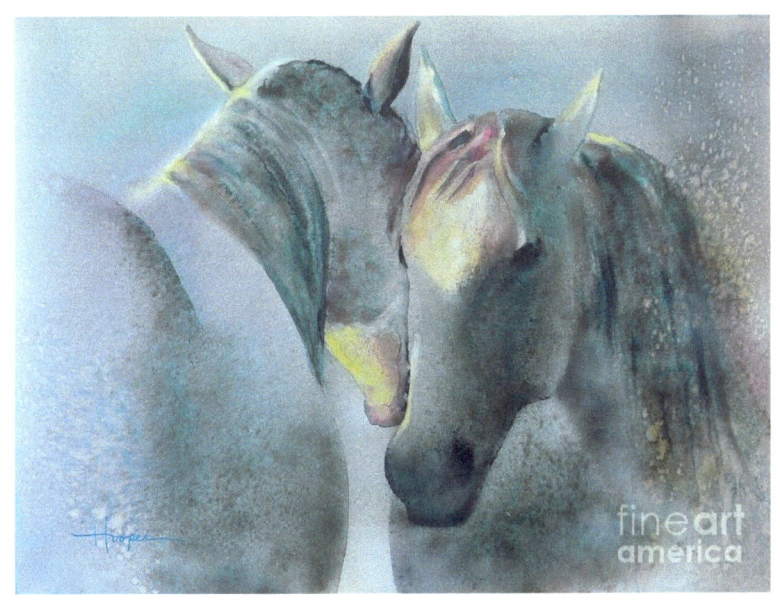

Winter Lovers

Robert Hooper

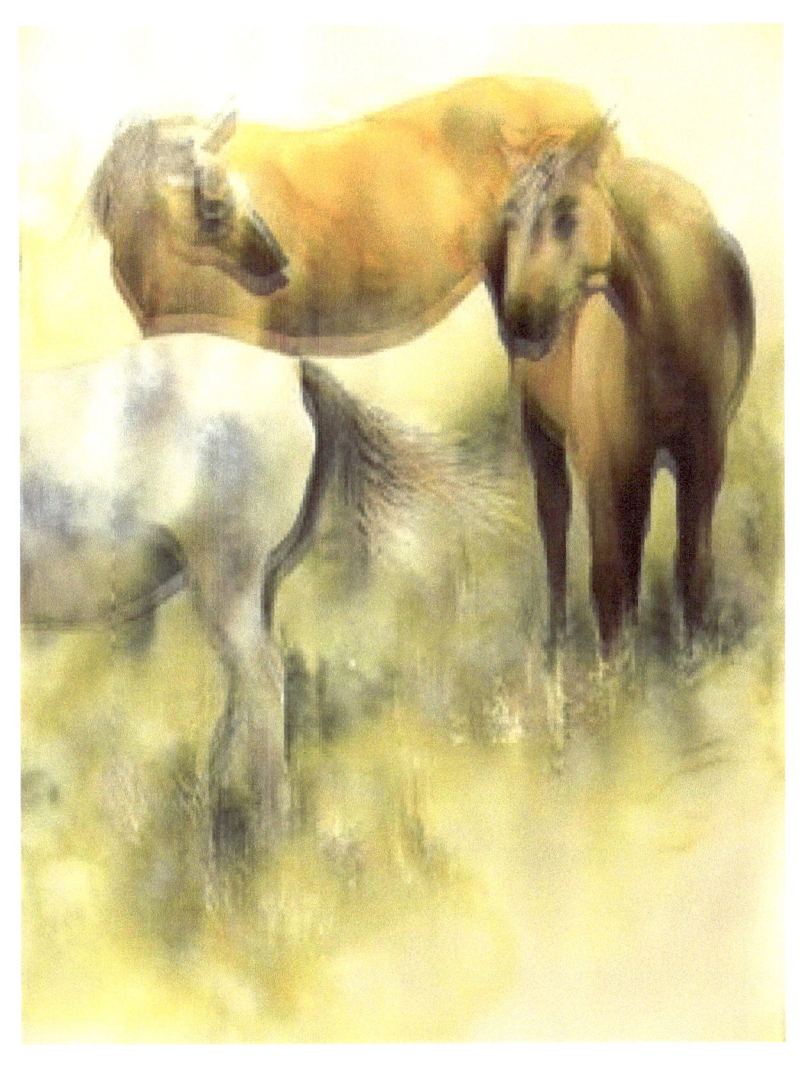

Just Looking

Robert Hooper

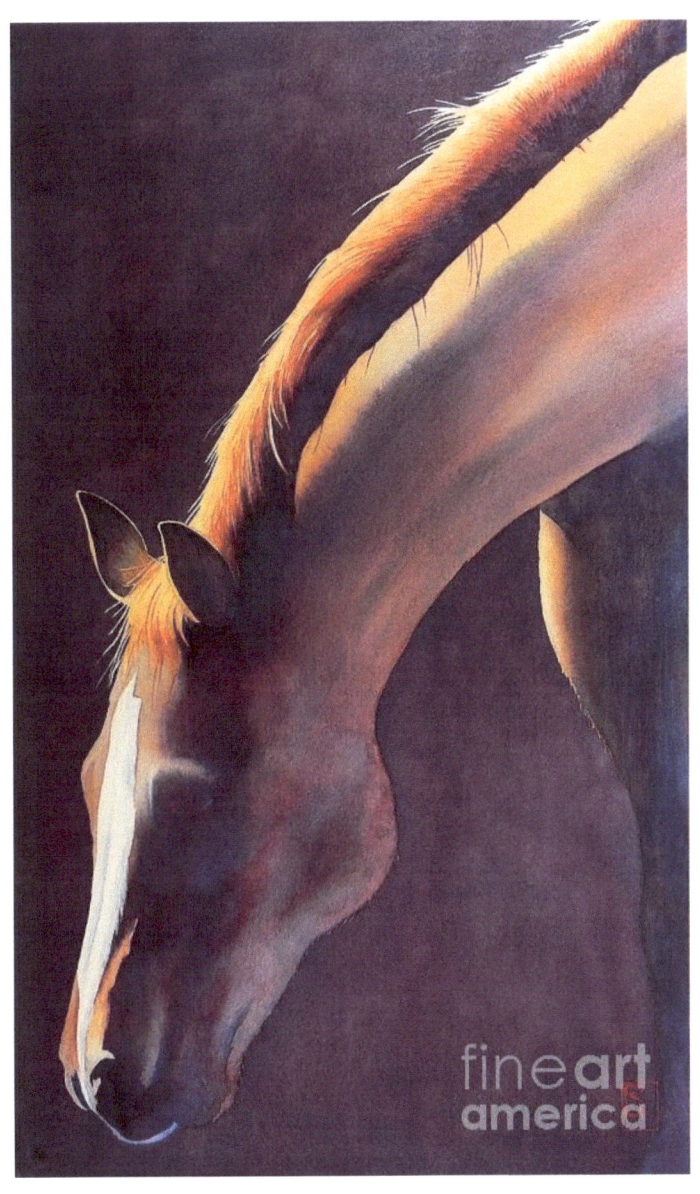

Dollar Painting

Robert Hooper

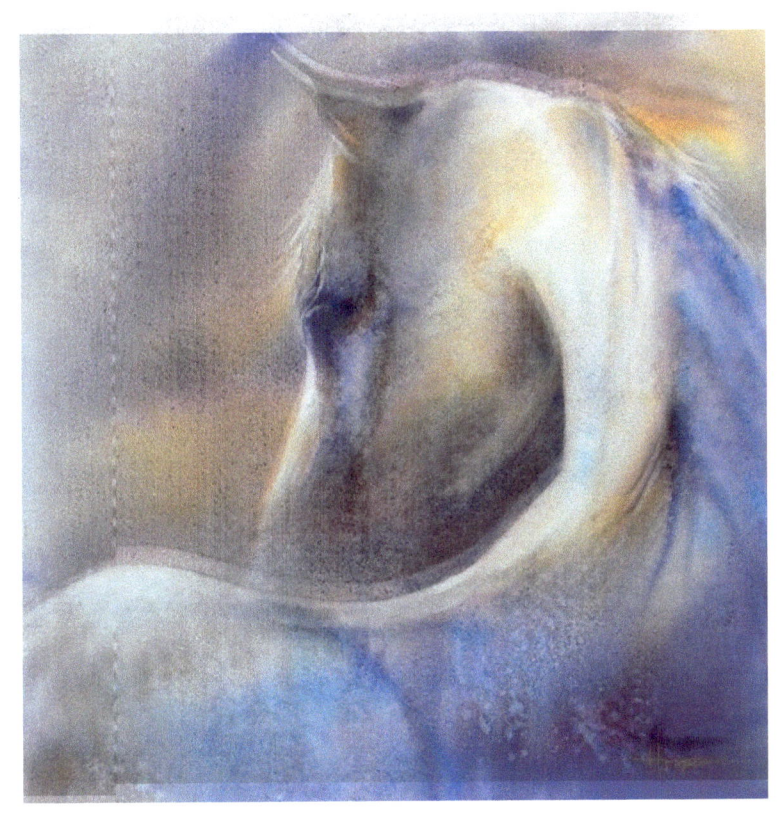

Behold

Robert Hooper

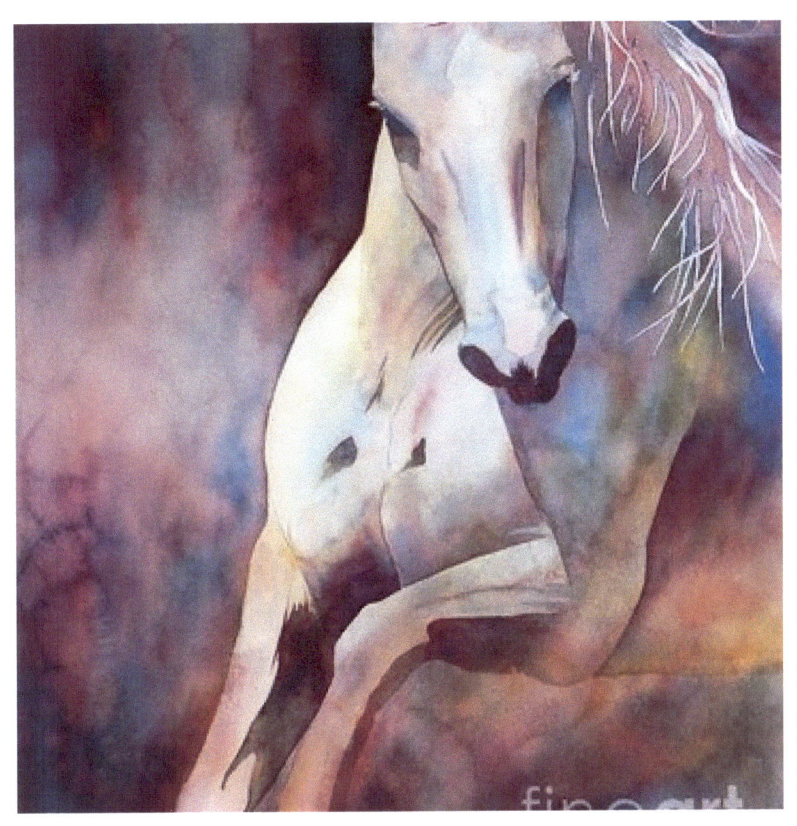

Spirit

Robert Hooper

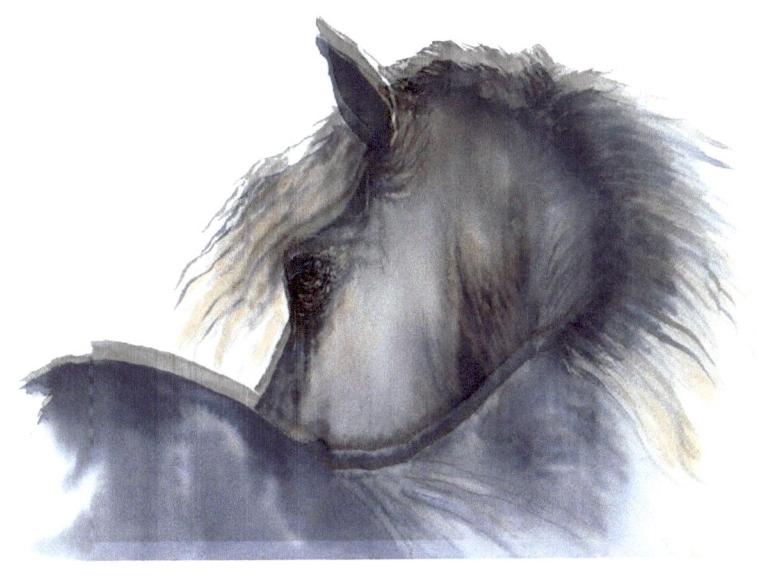

Watercolor Horse

Robert Hooper

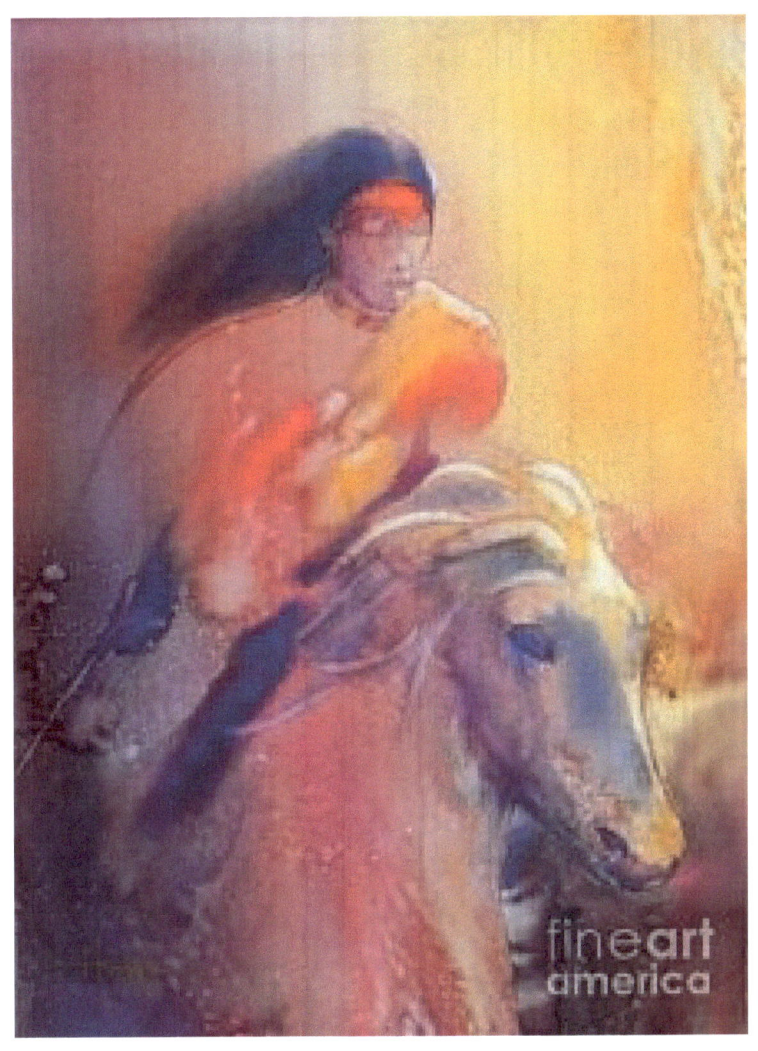

Fire Horse

Robert Hooper

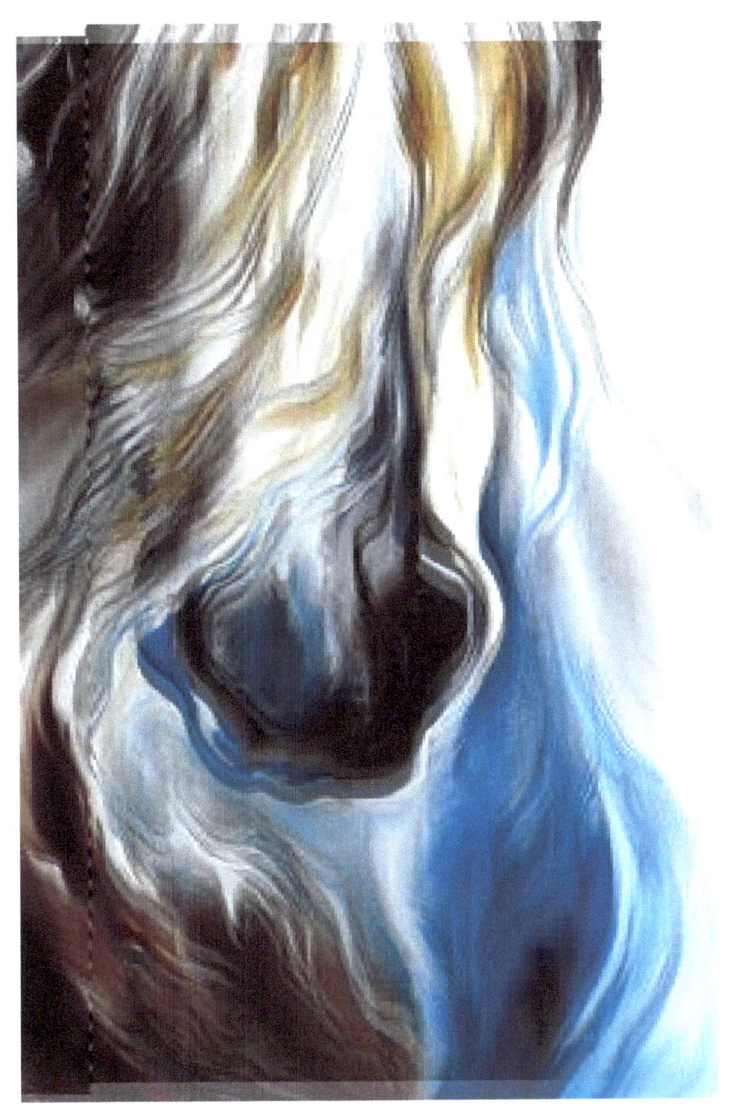

Spirit Horse

Robert Hooper

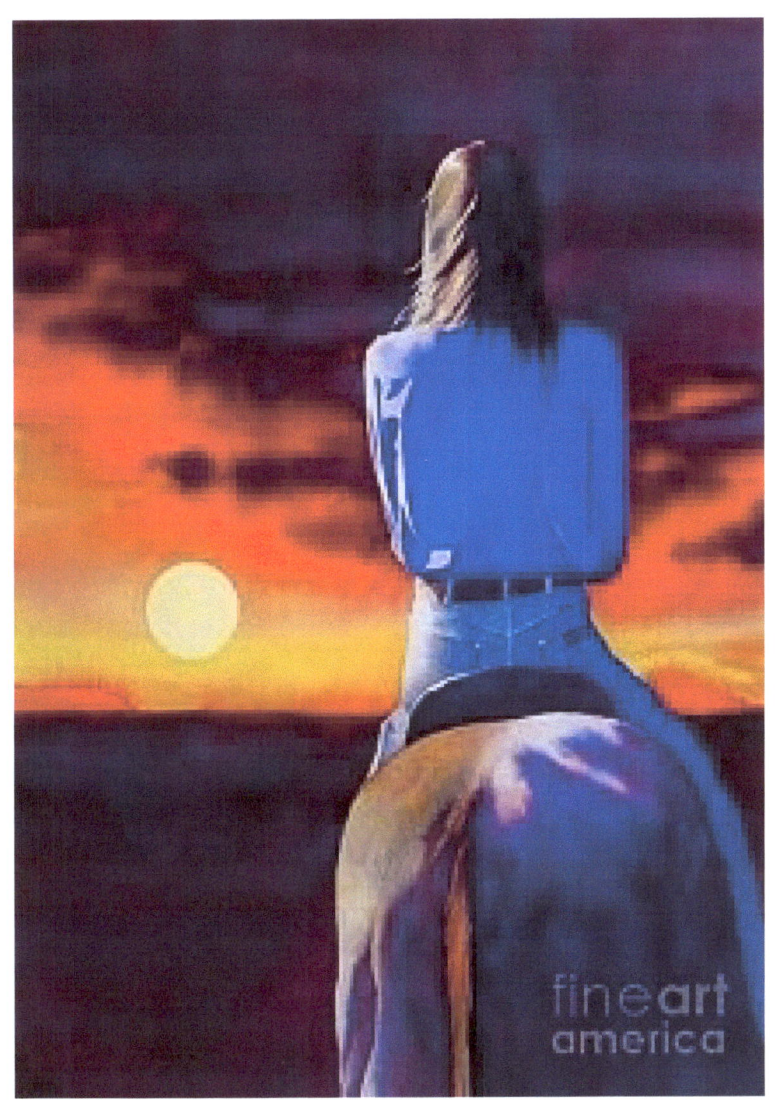

Looking West

Robert Hooper

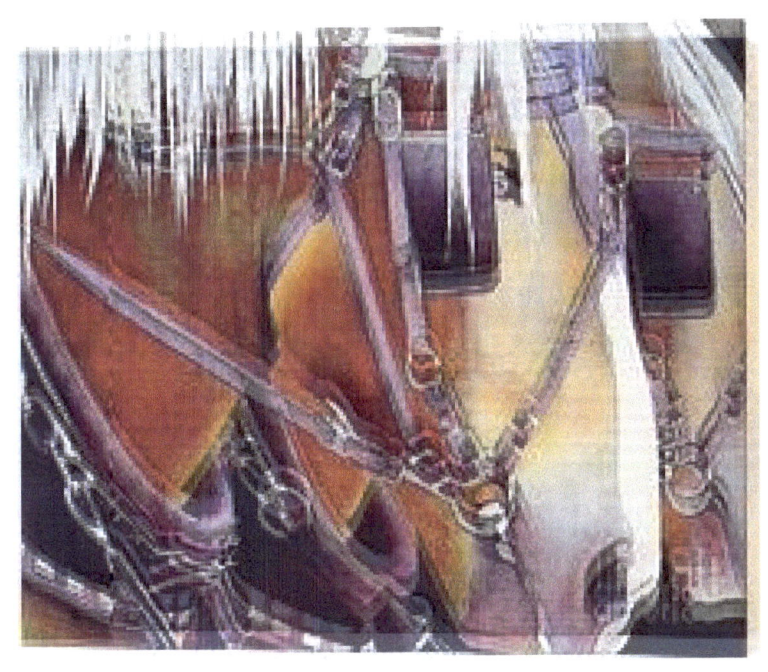

Farm Horses

Robert Hooper

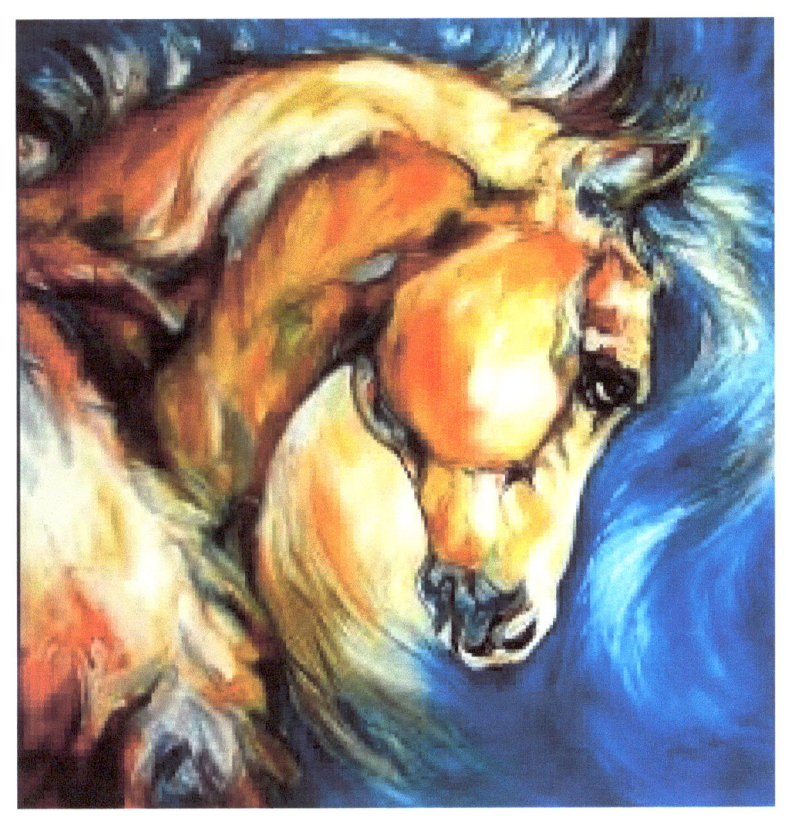

Kanthaka

Robert Hooper

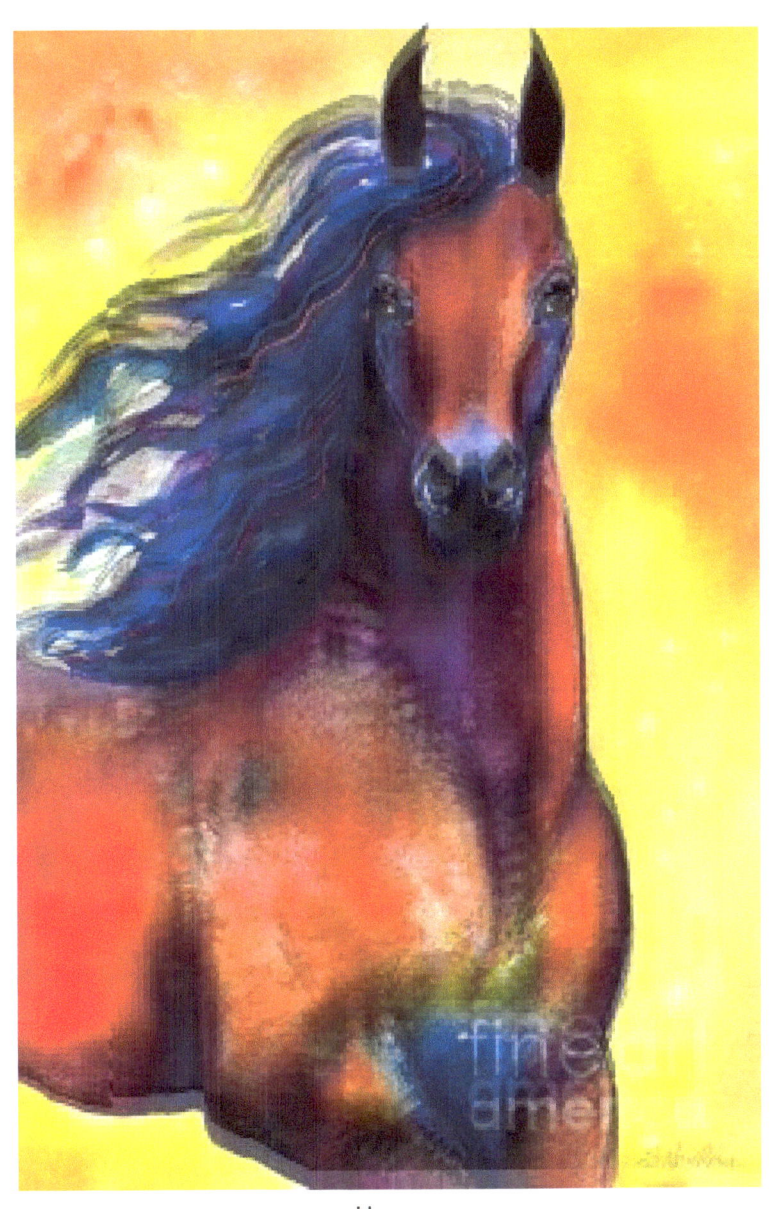

Horse

Robert Hooper

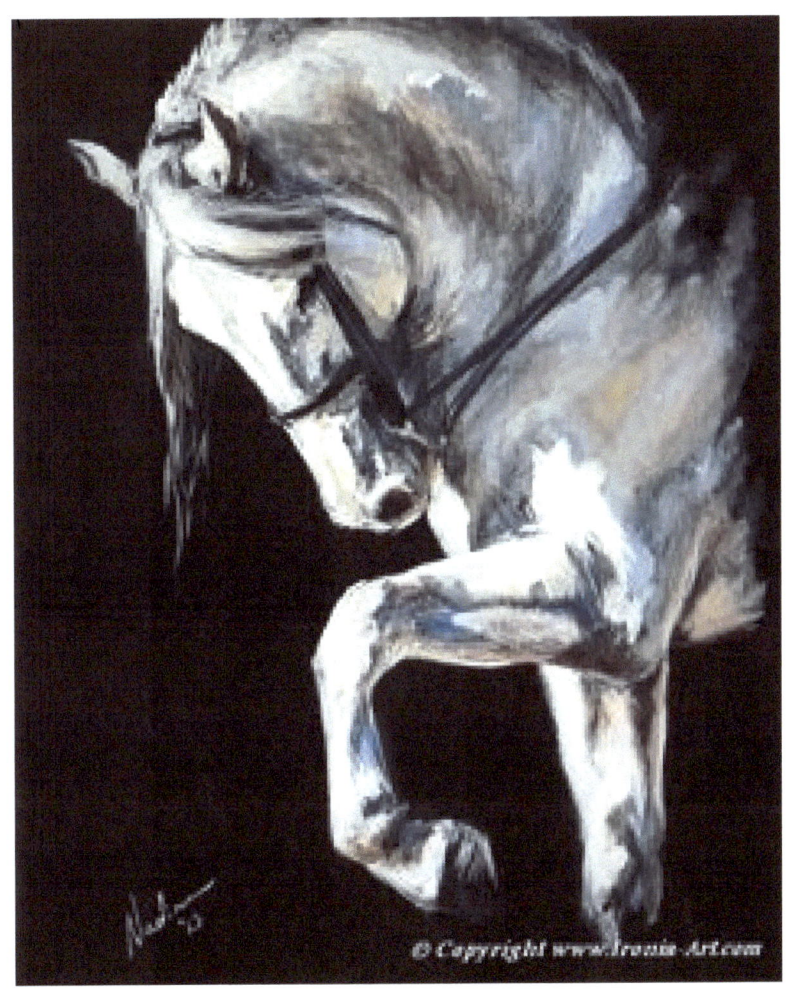

Horse

Robert Hooper

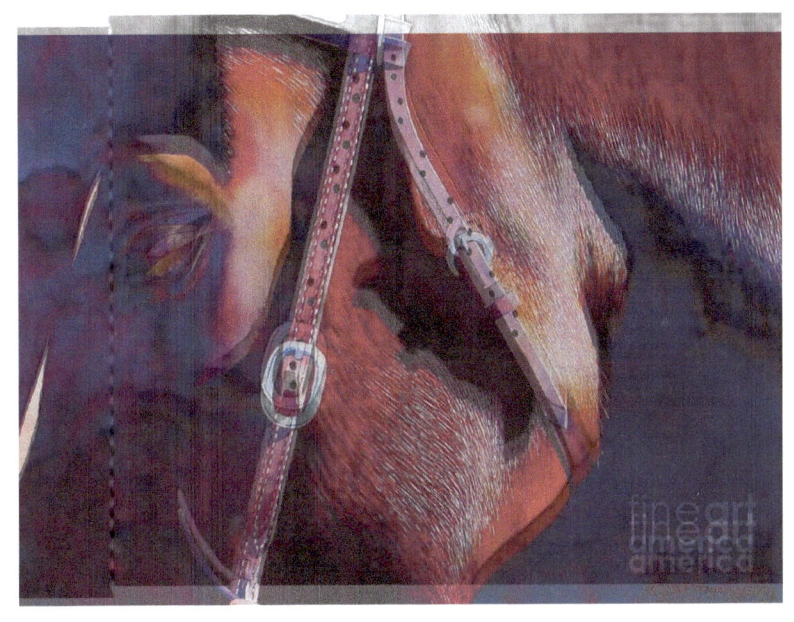

Horsepower

Robert Hooper

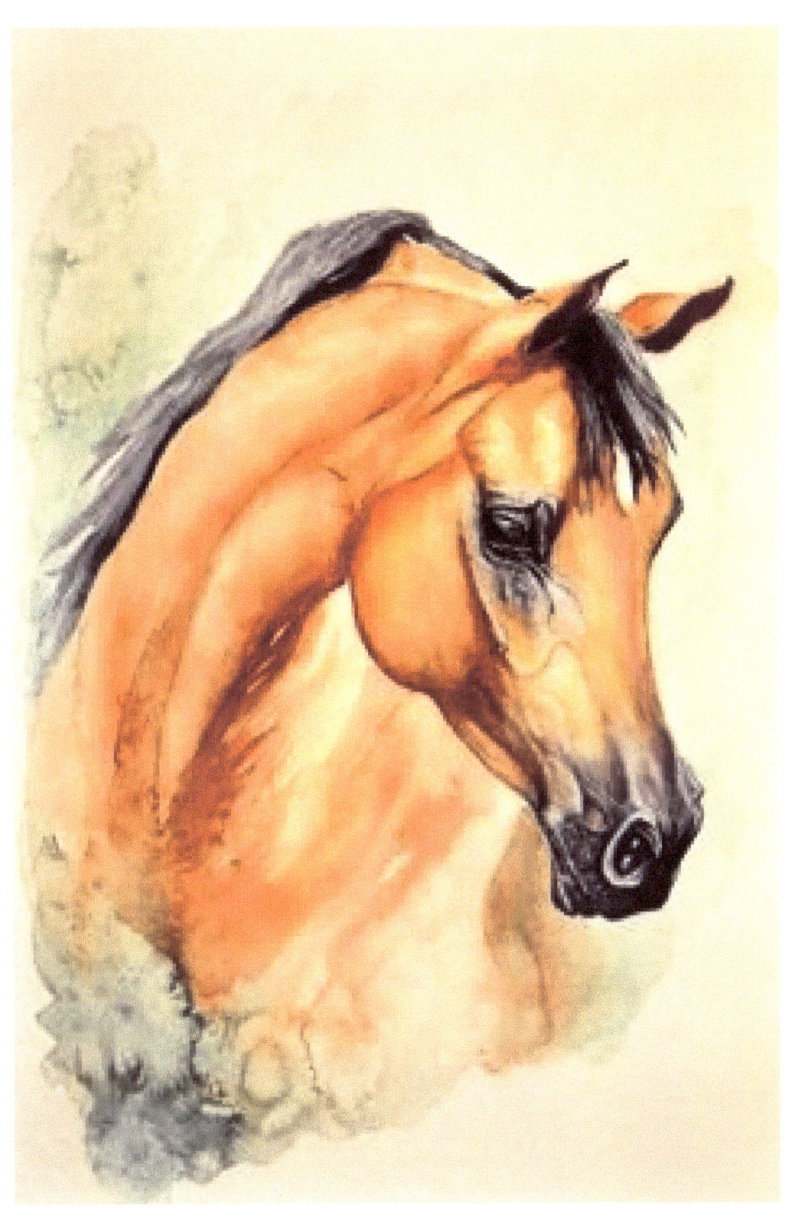

Aquarelle

Robert Hooper

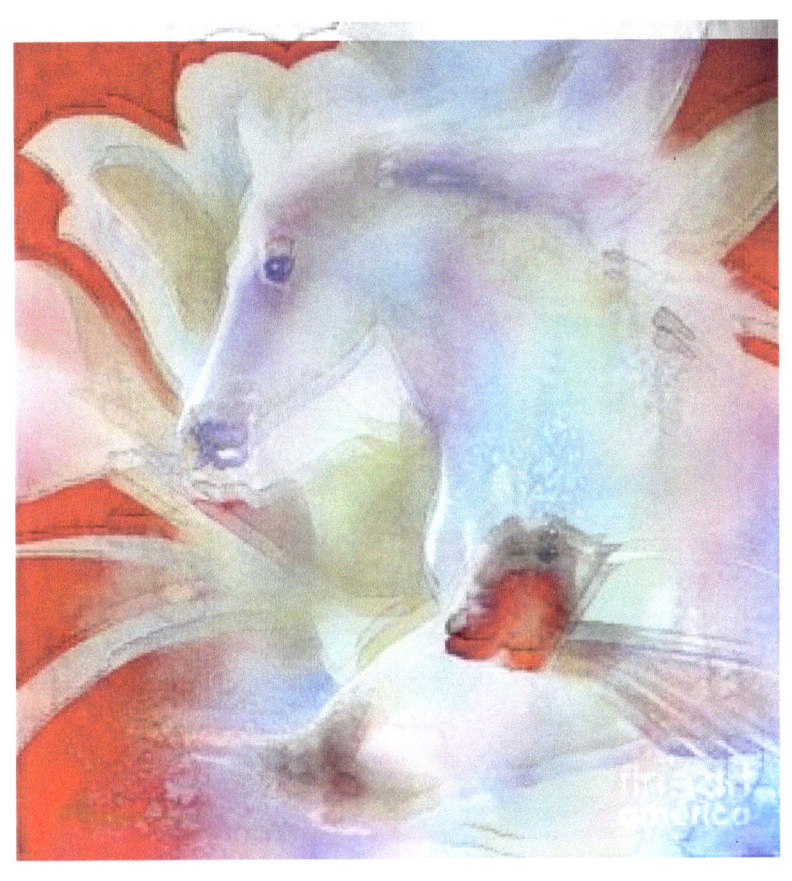

Dream

Robert Hooper

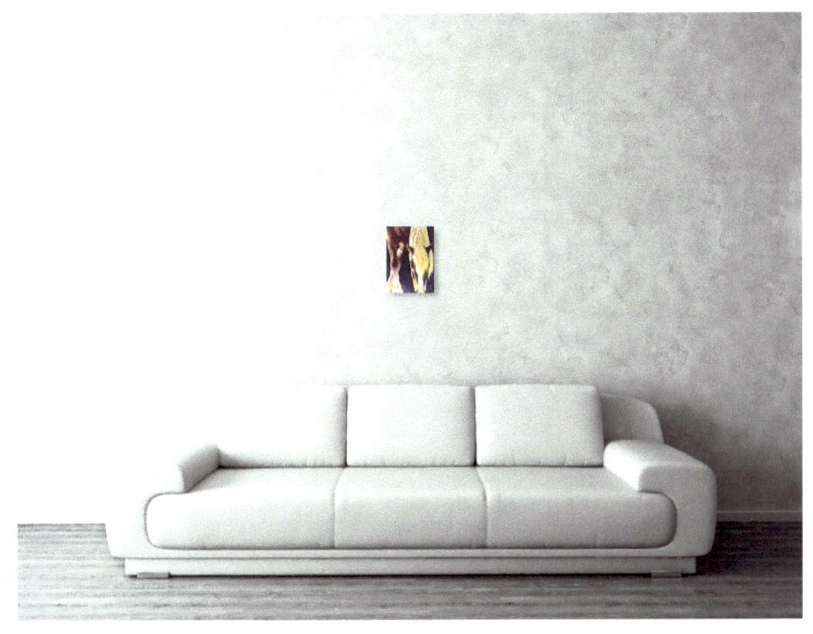

Eat Like a Horse Print

Robert Hooper

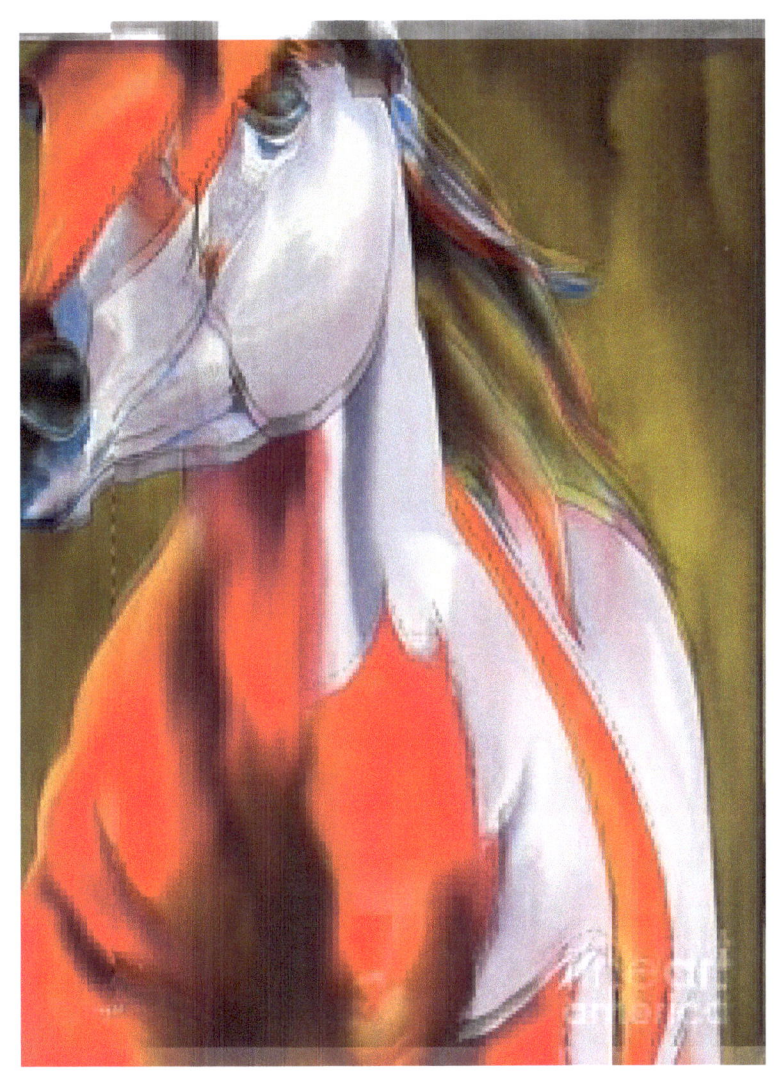

Fury

Robert Hooper

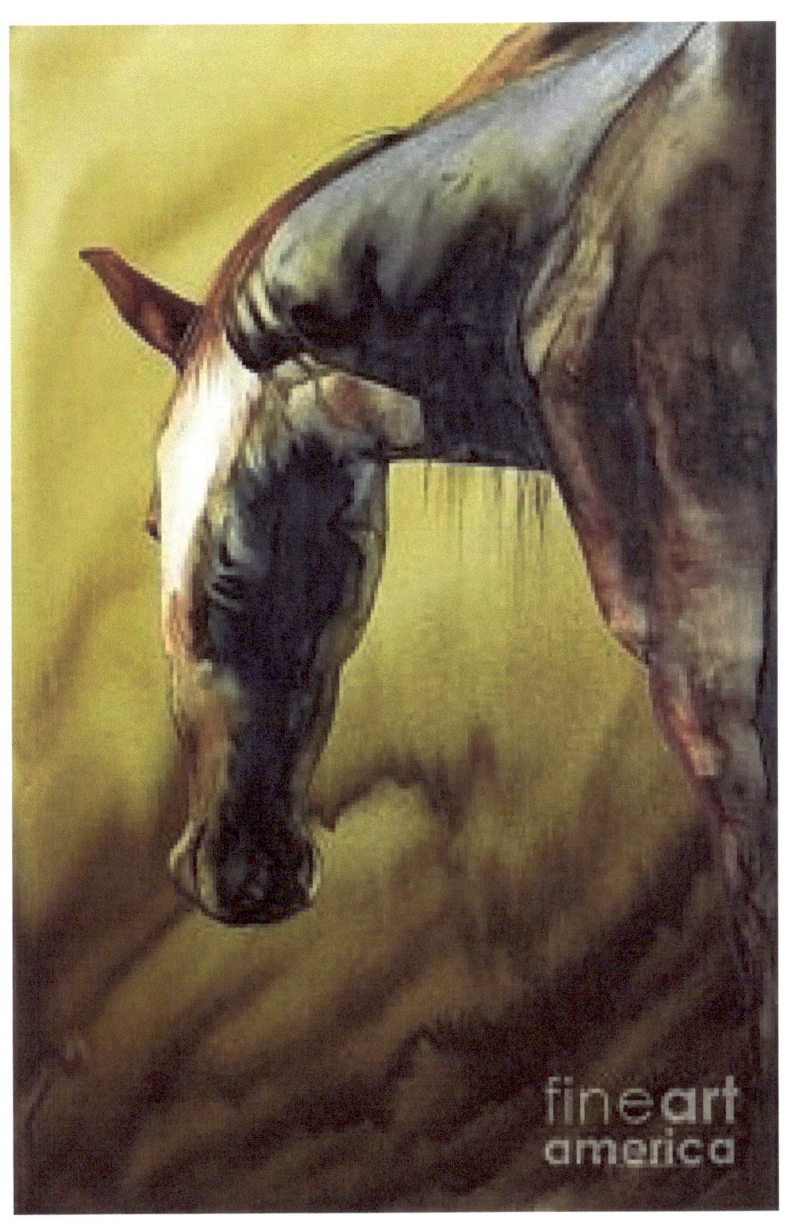

A Hard Day's Night

Robert Hooper

www.ingramcontent.com/pod-product-compliance
Lightning Source LLC
Chambersburg PA
CBHW051920210526
45473CB00006B/2081